D1686088

The Dragon's Tale
and Other Children's Poems

Kevin Bowe

The Dragon's Tale
and Other Children's Poems

Kevin Bower

ATHENA PRESS
LONDON

The Dragon's Tale and Other Children's Poems
Copyright © Kevin Bower 2007

All Rights Reserved

ISBN 10-digit: 1 84748 084 5
ISBN 13-digit: 978 1 84748 084 2

First Published 2007 by
ATHENA PRESS
Queen's House, 2 Holly Road
Twickenham TW1 4EG
United Kingdom

Printed for Athena Press

Contents

The Dragon's Tale

I woke up this morning but not in my home;
I was in a mystical place where unicorns roam,
Where dragons tell tales of sailors so tragic
Where witches and warlocks misuse their magic.
I found myself cold and strangely alone
Walking a path composed of charred stone,
When out of the trees came a great ball of fire
And a dragon politely bid me 'Good evening, sire'.
I asked where I was, with an increasing fear,
But the dragon looked puzzled and said, 'You are
    here.'
So I replied, 'How do I get home?'
'For that,' said the dragon, 'you'll need three stones.'
The dragon, he stood up to his full height
And told me a tale of an incredible fight
'A night,' said he, 'of merciless killing,
Of inhuman murder and excessive blood-spilling.
The men in the village were killed in their sleep
Never to wake from their slumber so deep.
The stones, they were taken up the mountain so
    steep,
To stay in the castle for the Emperor to keep.
You must get the stones and rub them together

Or you'll not see your home again, not now, not
    ever.'
I set off down the path with a feeling of dread,
The words of the dragon still in my head.
The mountain went high, up through the clouds;
I passed on through the shrimmering shrouds,
But soon I was there, at the side of a moat,
With water so deep I needed a boat.
Then, there on the shore, I caught sight of a mast.
A small sailing boat; it would get me there fast.
Before I knew it, I was climbing the wall,
Higher and higher, it was incredibly tall.
Into the castle, I looked for the stones,
Down corridors and parapets, I worked to the bone.
At last there they were, on a cushion blood-red
And the dragon's words returned to my head.
I rubbed them together, rubbing so hard,
My attention distracted, I did not hear the guard.
To my great surprise I was immediately jailed,
My attempt to get home was suddenly failed!

All through the night, I thought of a plan
To make good my escape, if only I can.
Try as I might, I could not move a bar
But to my amazement the door was ajar.
I got hold of the stones and rubbed them so hard,
Found myself back on the path that was charred.
And there was the dragon that had helped me
    before.
'Now it's time,' he said, 'to even the score.
Give me the stones and be on your way
Perhaps you'll return here another day.'

Then I woke up, I was back in my bed,
Remembering the words the dragon had said.
So, perhaps everything was not as it seemed
And I'd see the dragon again, tonight in my dreams.

The Island Lullaby

I've heard tales of a distant land,
Where monsters roam so big and grand:
Some with fur, some with scales,
Some that fly and have two tails.
So one day I thought I'd take a trip,
I hired a crew and bought a ship.
For two long years we were out at sea:
A parrot, a mermaid, the crew and me.
Yes, I did say a mermaid – all those myths are true.
I've met a Cyclops and a centaur and even a griffin
    or two.

Finally we found it – with cliffs up to the sky,
The first men in one thousand years to set foot on
    Lullaby.
The island was mostly jungle with a generous share
    of lakes,
We battled past the dinosaurs, the vampires and
    snakes.
In the middle of the island, no one could have
    known,
We found a noble monarch, sitting on his throne.
I told him of our journey, our adventures and our
    fears,

But the king did not reply for he'd been dead for many years.
It was a statue that was sat upon the regal throne,
A mannequin of rock; no longer skin and bone.
We looked around his chambers to find treasure and lots more,
But all we found downstairs was a tight-locked dungeon door.
I knew we had to open it or regret it to our grave,
Some of my crew scampered off, they were not so brave.
We opened up the door, moved it oh so wide,
With fear and trepidation, we took a step inside.

There before our eyes, we couldn't believe what we had found,
A beautiful fair-haired princess lying still upon the ground.
Beside her was a plaque with its own tale to tell,
Of how she'd been there ten score years, deep under a spell.
And by the tale a phrase which had to be read aloud,
So I took a breath, cleared my throat, and stood up proud.
'Under a spell for many years, never again to wake.
Now she's found, I stand my ground and see the spell to break.'
I raised the plaque above my head and crashed it to the floor,

The princess started moving and opened her eyes
   once more.
We sat talking for hours, she told me of her woe,
Of how the king we thought was dead was indeed
   her greatest foe.
She said he was a danger and not to look into his
   eyes,
For he was not a normal man, but evil in disguise.

I got my men together and went back to find the
   king
But there was nothing left of him, not a single
   thing.
I talked amongst my men, they didn't want to die,
We thought it best to swiftly leave the island
   Lullaby.
We ran as fast as possible, all the way to the boat,
We rubbed our eyes, to our surprise, the thing was
   still afloat.
As we prepared to sail away, the evil king stood in
   our way,
Lightning bolts he threw at our bow
We struggled to get away somehow.

Before we could even set the sail,
Out of the waves leapt a giant whale,
With just one swipe of his mighty tail
He sent the king to surf and shale.
Our mermaid helped with her humpback friend
And brought the king to a watery end,
We fixed the boat and bid goodbye
To the mysterious island Lullaby.

Wasaplace

There is a place called Wasaplace
I know you won't believe,
That is until I tell you
The tale of little Eve.

Now Eve she was a poor girl
Whose desire was to roam,
But instead she had to live with her mother
In their humble little home.

Eve woke up one morning,
Longing for open space
So she packed a bag and headed out
To locate Wasaplace.

Carrying a bag of savoury goods,
Eve found herself at Wasaplace Woods.
Two paths to choose, which way to go?
Which way was safe? Eve didn't know.

Then she heard a great booming voice,
'Which way to go? You must make a choice.'
Eve turned around and what she saw,
Was a giant, scaly, razor-sharp claw.

Ten claws in total, Eve looked up so high,
A fire-breathing dragon was scaling the sky.
'I'll tell you the right way, which way to choose,'
Boomed down the dragon, *'what have you to lose?'*

'My thanks, Mr Dragon, but how can I repay?'
The dragon looked down, *'Now hear what I say.*
On the far side of the woods you'll find a small house,
In the darkest corner, you'll find a small mouse.
Bring me that mouse and our debt is repaid,
Now take the path that lies in the shade.'

The path through the woods was dark and scary,
Eve ran from ogres, demons and fairies.
The ground where she walked was beaten and worn,
Trampled by minotaur and unicorn.

Vampire bats flew around her head
As deeper into the woods little Eve fled.
Eve ran faster and fell to the ground,
Looking up it was a house she found.

Eve stepped forward, through the door,
And walked across a creaky floor.
'Hello,' she called, her voice filled the house;
'Hello,' came back, the voice of a mouse.
Eve said that the dragon had sent her, they really should go,
But the mouse said that first there was something to know.

'Listen to me child, I have a story to tell,
I wasn't always a mouse, I'm under a spell.
An evil witch made me so small
And made my husband a dragon so tall.
If you can get the two of us to unite
Once again all shall be right.'

A few hours later the door opened wide,
The evil witch stepped in.
Eve ran, the witch was knocked off her feet,
She fell to the floor in crumpled defeat.
While the witch was down they ran through the
    door,
Into Wasaplace Woods, Eve running once more.
Out of the woods, Eve and the mouse ran
To once again be with her man.

Then he was there, way up in the sky
'*My wife!* with a puff of smoke the dragon did cry.
Eve fell to the ground in a blazing light,
When she opened her eyes they were there in her
    sight.
A happy young couple, united through smoke
United forever, the spell had been broke.

They passed on their thanks as Eve climbed to her
    feet,
She was just thankful the witch had been beat.
They asked if Eve would return this way,
She said, 'No thanks, I've had enough for today.'
And so she set off at a blistering pace
To tell her mum the story of that perilous place.

So now perhaps you may believe
In the adventures of a girl called Eve,
And all the dangers she had to face
In that place called Wasaplace.

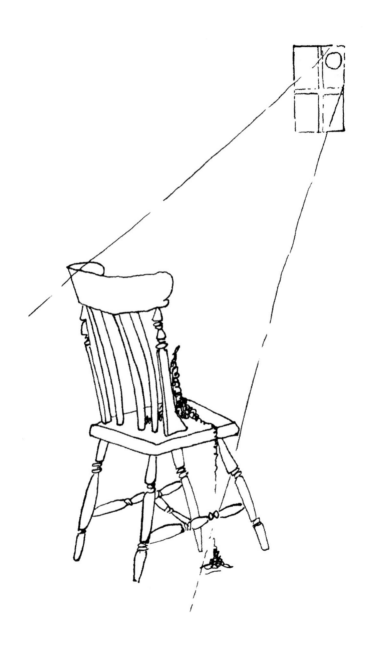

The Night Prowler

Born so long ago, in such a darkened time,
It's not his fault that he's guilty of crime.
Barely a boy when the attack first occurred,
From master to pupil the evil was transferred.

The branch was broken from the family tree,
A real bad seed, to the nights he would flee.
He had no heart just a void in its place
As cold and dark as the far reaches of space.

Deep in his soul he knew he would feed,
Out all night, he would fulfil his need.
Every night this would happen, the unexplained
  killing;
Men, women, and children; all their blood spilling.

The law was confused, outwitted and baffled,
The mysterious murders they couldn't unravel.
The seasons they changed and the years went by,
Still the innocent continued to die.

The police were no wiser up till this time,
Just who was guilty of these terrible crimes.
Hundreds were dead and still not a clue,
Who was killing these people, nobody knew.

He lived by his own rules, he lived by the night.
He knew he was wrong but still it felt right.
He opened the windows and climbed on in,
Again to commit the ultimate sin.

There was a scent in the air, the essence of willow,
Then he saw her pretty head on the pillow.
She looked so tranquil, she looked so fine;
Tonight, he would find somewhere else to dine.

He stayed there for hours just watching her face.
Perfectly still and so full of grace.
He looked at her neck and she opened her eyes.
He stared right in them, tonight nobody dies.

He leapt through the curtains, to the shadows he
   fled,
Leaving the beauty to dream in her bed.
He cried in the darkness, unloved and alone,
Would there ever be anyone to have for his own?

Many a month has flown dismally by
Since they had met and she opened her eyes.
His visions were haunted by the sight of her face,
So night after night he returned to that place.

He'd made up his mind, he wanted a wife,
But to make her his own, he must take her life.
He pulled back the covers and prepared to go to it.
He choked back the tears, he just couldn't do it.

A life must be taken but it would not be she,
'I shall take my own life, it must be me.

He sat at the window and watched the sun rise,
As everyone knows, that's how a vampire dies.

The lady awoke just after dawn,
She closed the window with a stretch and a yawn.
As she stood there it was as though someone had
    died.
She felt all alone but she didn't know why.

The killings had stopped and after some time,
The police gave up the unsolvable crime.
And as for the lady it would take her a while,
To get over seeing a vampire smile.

David

It was a shame for little David
Because no one ever liked him.
He was very ugly, smelt a lot,
And was more than just a bit dim.
But he didn't help himself,
He kept taking things that weren't his own,
Then he made a big mistake
By taking someone else's garden gnome.
This made everybody hate him
And everyone was mad,
So David had to run away
And nobody was sad!

Reggie Yates

Allow me to introduce myself, my name is Reggie Yates;
I'll tell you where I'm going, and it ain't the Pearly Gates!
You see I've been a sinner, a good man I am not;
The place that I am going to, be sure it's pretty hot!

I've robbed banks and burnt out cars, even been known to kill,
And the reason that I did it? Boy was it a thrill!
I've always been a villain, through life and now to death;
So now I lie here dying, a bullet in my chest.

Now I'll tell you this, as the darkness closes in,
Life just isn't living if you live from sin to sin.
Now the light has passed me, and I can feel the heat,
Reggie Yates and Satan, wouldn't that be neat!

A Little Magic

A little boy walked down the street one day
With a skip in his step singing hip hip hooray.
When out of the bushes a monster did crawl,
The boy took out a wand and turned him to a ball,
He kicked it over a hill and into a river
Where the monster turned back and escaped with a
    shiver.

The little boy kept walking and what did he see?
A vampire coming and ready to feed.
The little boy thought it would be so much fun
If he could turn himself into the sun.
The vampire screamed and really took flight,
He didn't like day; he much preferred night.

As the boy walked on, a werewolf arrived,
He threw him a bone and the young boy survived.
Round the corner near home, a giant gorilla!
'Some magic bananas there, that'll fill ya!'
When he went home his mum said 'Are you all
    right?'
The boy jumped in the air, 'Mum, you gave me a
    fright!'

The Queen of Nowhere

On a dark, gloomy night, to the great hall I was
   beckoned.
My name is in full Theodore the Second.
The reason for my calling, it meant trouble or that's
   what I reckoned,
And so it was proved on this miserable night,
Against all my wishes, I was proved to be right.
For there on the sofa was my master, near death,
He called me close, he was gasping for breath.
'I have an adventure for you, one not to fail.
I'm sending you to quest for the Holy Grail;
The cup of Christ, lost for thousands of years.'
Then he breathed his last and I shed a few tears.
And even before he'd been laid to rest
I was on a plane heading due west
To the Holy Land where the Grail lay,
Waiting to be found again one day.

I hired a guide to take me over the sand,
Thousands of miles of the Holy Land.
We found a temple that was falling apart,
The guide told me that here we should start.
We saw on a wall some mysterious glyphs
Which when translated turned our beliefs into
   myths.

There was no such thing as the Grail we sought,
All of our troubles had been for nought.
We followed the story upon the wall
To see which place we next should call.

Far across the seven seas,
Beneath a canopy of the tallest trees,
There is an island and no one goes there,
Known to all as the Isle of Nowhere.
Rumour has it that dangers lurk near
And mythical creatures go berserk here.

So to this island we set sail
To find what we could, but not the Grail.
The myth was unclear of what was there,
But we'd take the chance, we had to dare.
We prepared ourselves for trials and shocks
As we manoeuvred our ship between the rocks.
Our sails were up and soon we'd blow there
To the uncharted place, the Isle of Nowhere.

With a final gust we were well within reach
And the ship crashed up onto the beach.
We set off on foot: me, my guide and the crew,
Not sure what to think, much less what to do.
Then within fifty yards of where our ship had
    been grounded
We found ourselves completely surrounded.
Island natives we just hadn't seen,
We were gagged and bound in front of their
    queen.

'Arise,' she said to me and my guide.
And cautiously she took us aside.
'What is your business, why are you here?'
We told her our tale of how the tale was unclear.
'The Grail of Christ! Is that what you're after?'
Then the great hall was filled with laughter.
'My dear chaps, you must be unstable,
For the reason you're here is merely a fable.
So now I believe that you must have been lying,
As intruders in Nowhere you will be doing some
dying.
You will take your chances in our mighty arena
Against Dart the dragon, there is simply no
meaner!'

Within the hour we were given a shield and a sword
To take on the dragon, scaly fire-lord.
A large gate rose up, higher and higher,
Out stepped Dart, breathing huge balls of fire.
We all ran for cover away from the flames,
Trying to survive these dastardly games.
One man threw a spear but it soared over Dart's
head,
Hitting the wall and the floor, missing its target
instead.
I ran at the dragon and struck with my blade,
No cut, no mark, no indent was made.
Dart lashed out with his mighty front claw,
Several feet through the air I really did soar.
My guide dashed towards Dart, showing no fear,
While I ran the other way grabbing the spear.
My guide, like myself, was thrown ever higher,

And the dragon stood tall, breathing out fire.
I took hold of the spear and stabbed through the
   heart,
No more to bellow the once mighty Dart
With a last puff of smoke he fell to the ground,
All round the arena no one made a sound.

The queen was angry, for Dart was her pet,
She'd take out her fury on us, you can bet.
'Into the jungle, you must run for your lives,
For my men will be chasing, yielding spears and
   knives.'
So that's how it was if we wished to be free,
We must run for our lives through the densest of
   trees.
The natives gave no chance, we had no head start,
The man to my right went down with a dart.
The rest of us ran, the trees became blurred,
The natives gave chase but never were heard.
One by one my crew hit the ground,

Spears, swords and darts, but never a sound.
Then only two left, just me and my guide,
All of my crew had needlessly died.
On we both ran and fell to our knees,
Because into our faces came a sea breeze.
We ran down the beach, to the ship, to survive,
Not even knowing if we'd make it alive.

When we had made it, we stood on the deck,
Never before been so proud of our wreck.
The queen had arrived, her eyes full of hate

'So you have managed to escape Heaven's gate.
I grant you your lives, this I decree,
But now we return to our home in the sea.'
The Isle of Nowhere, the queen and her slaves,
Started to shake and sank into the waves.

Atlantis was Nowhere, an island with a name,
They shared the same place; they were one and the
    same.
That's why the wall was unclear in its meaning,
The Isle of Nowhere was not what it's seeming.
The Isle of Nowhere means something to me
Because the island is somewhere deep in the sea.

Thirty-first Century

An iceberg meteor headed for Earth,
A serious matter, no time for mirth.
None of the boffins knew what to do,
None of the scientists had even a clue.
If Earth was hit by this thing from space
It would mean the end of the human race.
So it was decided to blow it to pieces,
The only way to save our species.

They looked for someone to fly the rocket,
To go to space to try and stop it.
Captain Smith heard of the monster of ice,
To save the planet they didn't ask twice.
He climbed aboard his spaceship so fast,
He sat and waited, ready to blast.

Then he was off, faster than light,
Ready to put up such a good fight.
For thousands of miles he flew by his wits,
Prepared to blow that iceberg to bits.
Then at last with the meteor in sight,
He punched the bomb button with all of his might.

But the bomb button came off in his hand,
Things were not going as well as he'd planned.

There was nothing else for it, the rocket must crash,
He flew into the meteor with an almighty smash.
The berg was destroyed but Smith shed no tears
For he was frozen in ice for one thousand years.

For an entire millennium he sailed on through
    space,
The same frozen look stuck on his face.
The rocket crash-landed making animals run,
The ice soon melted by the heat of the sun.
Smith started to stir and opened his eyes,
He got to his feet and stared at the skies.

The sky was red, no longer blue,
So totally different to the sky that he knew.
He was starting to wonder just where he'd arrived,
He was beginning to doubt that he'd even survived.
A good look around showed no cars or a tree,
In fact, all around there was nothing to see.

But through his ship's radar Smith could read
A large cloud of dust gathering speed.
People, he thought, it just has to be
A rescue mission coming for me.
People it was on a vehicle of steel;
Smith pinched himself to make sure it was real.

Four in total, they pulled him to the ground.
He put up a good fight but he was soon gagged and
    bound.
For many miles he was dragged behind,
The sand was burning, the sun making him blind.

They finally stopped and sank into the sand,
Miles below they hit solid land.

'What have you done? Why am I here?
What do you want? What is the year?'
Out of the sun, Smith was now cooler,
When a door slid open and in stepped their ruler.
'Three thousand and seven, my dear Captain Smith,
I can't believe you are here, I thought you a myth.'

A thousand years gone! Smith couldn't believe what
  he'd heard,
Everything here was completely absurd.
All family and friends lost in the past.
How could it be? It happened so fast.
Smith fell to his knees, incredibly sad,
All of his feelings driving him mad.

'My good Captain Smith, my name is Meat,'
The leader came close, helped him up to his feet.
'Your experience is invaluable, you see we need
  your aid.
Meteors keep hitting us. That's why we're here in
  the shade.
But a meteor is heading here, by far the biggest yet.
If you can help destroy it, we are forever in your
  debt.

'We have repaired your rocket and you now can use
  your bomb,
If you can't destroy it then the human race will be
  gone.'

Smith shook him by the hand and looked him in the eye,
'Get me to my rocket and get me in the sky!'
Smith sat in his cockpit staring at the monster made of ice,
'Boy am I a hero, saving Earth not once but twice.'

Then Smith took off in a giant blaze of fire,
His spaceship going into space, climbing ever higher.
The meteor was in front of him, much bigger than before;
He hoped the bomb would do the job, he really wasn't sure.
He pushed the button to release it, then he felt quite sick.
Instead of the bomb flying out all he heard there was a click.

'Only one thing for it,' Smith's eyes filled up with tears.
'I wonder what the Earth will be like in one thousand years?'

The Rodeo Star

I ain't just the star of your rodeo
I'm more than a ride with no place to go.
Treat me even, treat me fair,
Treat me please, as though you care.

Because when I'm alone and stare into space
The stars they move and form your face.
So when I ask and you say 'no',
Think once again of your rodeo.

I ride the horses and brave the buck
In the hope you give me a glancing look.
I see you looking and I can tell you know
That I'm the star of your next rodeo.

I won your heart, I'm the best in the field,
My broken heart and scars now have healed.
Because I'm the man, the star of the show,
The hero in your very own rodeo.

He

I saw a man on the street, looked like he'd been there a while.

He looked up at me, shrugged his shoulders, gave me a nicotine smile.

He asked me where I was going, I said 'Just on my way,'

He told me that's the way to live, take it day by day.

He showed me pages of his diary, the good times now all faded.

The look in his eye, not never-say-die, just a poor man jaded.

He told me of his gambling days, living by the turn of a card;

He'd bet on black, it turned over red, and it hit him oh so hard.

The turn of a hand had cost him ten grand and then it cost him his wife.

She'd taken the house, she'd taken the kids and took the dignity out of his life.

He was now all alone, his name was unknown and that's the way he died.

Right to the end, I was his only friend and no matter what I tried,

It was such a big shame, I did not know his name; and that's the reason I cried.

The Bermuda Square

A plane above the ocean, soaring in the blue,
A strange, uncharted island coming into view.
Nobody knows about it, no one even knows it's
there,
The reason for the mystery? It's in the Bermuda
Square.

You may not know of it but you'll have heard about
its brother.
The triangle is one thing but the square is like no
other.
It has only one small island, found directly in the
middle;
Many boats and planes have gone, it really is a
riddle.

A plane above the ocean, soaring in the blue,
The instruments just went wild, what could a pilot
do?
He had no other option, he had to take it down,
He landed on what he thought was sand but was
really solid ground.

The plane was totally broken, well beyond repair,
The crew and all the passengers were suffering
   despair.
As they looked around them there were hundreds
   more smashed craft;
Surely out of all of them, they'd be able to make a raft.

They used ropes off ships and wings off planes,
Tied them up to make a frame.
They added seats from planes and wood from boats
Hoping it would stay afloat.

So they waded out into the waves,
Surely now they would be saved.
But just a few feet out at sea
The raft was turned and broke in three.

They all got back upon the beach,
Their freedom so far out of reach.
All the boats and planes that were on the ground
There were no survivors to be found.

What had happened? Where had they gone?
What on earth was going on?
The island was only tiny, really very small.
Where were the survivors? What happened to them
   all?

Then all around the island, as far as the eye could see,
Thousands of survivors, shrouded in mystery.
The captain took a step forward, feeling not so brave,
He waded out into the sea to those people from the
   waves.

After a few minutes, he came back upon the beach
To tell them what he had learnt and what they had
    to teach.
There was no way off the island, they had to live
    within the sea,
No other way around it, that's the way it had to be.

Looking around the island, they knew they had to
    leave,
If they went with the survivors, they would teach
    them how to breathe.
So they went with great regret and against their
    strongest wishes.
They went to live beneath the waves with all the
    sharks and fishes.

A plane above the ocean, soaring in the blue,
A strange uncharted island coming into view.

Match Day

Three o'clock on Saturday, the best time of the week,
I climb onto the terraces because that's where I like to shriek.
The match gets underway upon the stroke of three
With a shrill blast on the whistle blown by the referee.

The ball gets sent out wide and forward down the right,
Across up to the striker and he has the goal in sight.
He tries to chip the keeper but fails to make the most,
He sees the ball come back at him bouncing off the post.

Now there's a chance of counter as the ball comes flying back.
We must stand strong in defence as the opposing team attack.
They get the early ball in, our defender takes it on the head.
Now it's our turn to attack, '*Come on you Mighty Reds!*'

A swift, passing motion and the ball is in the bag.
Oh no! It can't be true, the linesman raised his flag.
Their keeper takes the kick and sends it flying high,
The midfield battle for it as though it's do or die!

The tackles go in hard to keep the movement going,
The ball runs loose wide on the left and goes out for
a throw-in.
Around the midfield line, the throw is high and
hard,
The defender goes in way too tough and gets a
yellow card.

A free kick to my team, just outside the D,
Our leading scorer starts his run, *Handball!* It has
to be.
The referee wastes no time in pointing to the spot;
The goalkeeper had no chance, the ball was burning
hot.

We're one-nil up at half time, with forty-five to
play;
We're going to have to keep the lead, not let it slip
away.
The second half is end to end, the midfield really
tight,
Then their player gets the ball and breaks quickly
down the right.

He gets the cross in early but our keeper makes the
claim;

He throws the ball out quickly and gets on with the game.
We're running down the middle but the striker's out too far,
He gives the ball a mighty kick and it sneaks under the bar.

The referee blows his whistle, the game is done, we're two-nil up.
Hooray! Yes! We've done it; *we've only won the cup!*

Whatnot

A seagull flies over the sea,
That's why he's called a seagull;
But if he flies over the bay
He isn't called a baygull.

Jack Russell is a little dog
Who sometimes enjoys cricket;
His legs are too short for him to bowl
So he's best behind the wicket.

A woodpecker does just that,
And a duck is known for bobbing;
So you'd better keep your money safe
If you see a robin.

You'll often see a lion
Lying on the ground.
An elephant makes a trunk call,
What an awful sound!

I've never climbed a molehill
Or skied a butter mountain;
I've never had my gob stopped
Or danced in a sherbet fountain.

Invasion

The fleet was massing on the far side of the sun,
No one yet knew the attack had begun.
They had travelled so far, faster than light,
Here to take Earth and ready to fight!
Aliens from a galaxy so far away,
An invasion so great, no one stood in their way.

Except Tommy Jones, just eight years old,
A small young boy coming down with a cold.
Early one morning he was walking to school,
He saw the ship land and their intention to rule.
A door slid open and out stepped some drones,
He ran and he hid, did young Tommy Jones!

But they soon found him, those creatures from
  space.
Tommy couldn't help it, he just sneezed in their face.
The creatures then sneezed and started to fall,
Back to their craft they proceeded to crawl;
Coughing and sneezing, they were not well at all.

The spaceship took off, up to the skies
Leaving young Tommy rubbing his eyes.
The aliens had come with weapons untold
Only to get beat by a boy's common cold.

A few days later, Tommy felt well,
But what of his encounter, who could he tell?

Kid Storm

Radiation! A mysterious thing,
Who knows what on earth it brings?
Certainly not young Jamie Strange
And how his life would forever be changed.

Jamie was out jogging one day
When a toxic truck was heading his way.
The truck itself wasn't so frightening,
That is until it was hit by lightning.

The lightning and truck hit Jamie together,
Changing his life now and forever.
Jamie woke up next morning in a hospital bed,
His leg was in plaster and a strap round his head.

The Doctor came round to see how he was feeling,
He couldn't believe it, he was already healing!
'I don't think you'll be needing that cast,
I've never known anyone to heal so fast.
I'll speak to my colleagues to see what we need.'
But Jamie ran off at phenomenal speed.

Jamie was shocked, he wanted to cry,
Hospital to home in the blink of an eye.
Somehow that truck had made him very quick,
He needed a costume, that's just the trick.

His mum made a suit; a new superhero was born;
Faster than light and they called him Kid Storm!
Jamie went to school and lived an average life
But Kid Storm would appear whenever there was
strife.

He would show up and accomplish his task,
No one knew who he was because of his mask.
They tried to take pictures but he was just way too
fast,
By the time they had clicked, the moment had
passed.

Who was the masked speedster? There were
rumours abound,
He'd come and he'd go, faster than sound.
Then one day from the far reaches of space,
To conquer the Earth, a huge robot race.

The robots were large, incredibly dangerous things
But Kid Storm appeared and began running rings.
The heat he created turned metal to mist;
All of the robots were quickly dismissed.

As it had been an earth-saving occasion,
Kid Storm stood still and let his picture be taken.
All over the news, across the nation,
Tales of heroics and his grand reputation.

Then one day Jamie's school caught on fire,
Never before a situation so dire!
Jamie ran and put on his suit,
To put out the fire was his pursuit.

Near the school there was a small lake,
His idea was a typhoon he could make.
He stood on the water to run as fast as he could,
Round and round in circles, to do what he should.

A typhoon started to grow, it went higher and higher,
Kid Storm led it to school and put out the fire.
Among the steam, with the building still warm,
Out stepped a hero, they called him Kid Storm.

Munchalot and Eatnowt

Sir Munchalot and Lord Eatnowt were going for
their dinner;
Sir Munchalot a hefty man, Lord Eatnowt much the
thinner.
They sat down at the table and waited for their
food,
Munchalot ordered everything but Eatnowt wasn't
in the mood.
Munchalot ate his burgers, breadsticks and his dip
While Eatnowt just sat there and nibbled on a chip.
Munchalot kept on going through his salad and his
steak,
Then he washed it all down with a cola and a shake.
Eatnowt thought he'd have dessert but decided not
to risk it;
Munchalot kept on going through his trifle and his
biscuits.
They moved into the lounge to enjoy a cup of
coffee,
Munchalot kept on going through chocolate mints
and then a toffee.
Munchalot had eaten so much he thought he might
be ill,

Then the waiter walked across and presented them
with a bill.
Munchalot kept on going and pushed the bill
towards Eatnowt;
Eatnowt pushed it back to Munchalot, what was
that about?

Mystical Sands

In the time of ancient Egypt, in days long gone by,
When shifting sands hold secrets and magic carpets
  fly.
An orphan boy lived on the streets begging to get
  some scraps,
Stealing if he had to then escape the Emperor's
  traps.

The Emperor was nasty, a really evil meanie,
He only got to be the emperor by virtue of a genie.
The orphan boy was captured, they asked of him his
  name,
He said he didn't have one, it really was a shame.

He was brought before the Emperor who said he
  had a quest.
The orphan boy declined and just laughed at the
  request.
While he was still laughing, a princess entered in,
The Emperor's lovely daughter who was not at all
  like him.

The Emperor stood tall and with his mighty voice:
'If you succeed at my request, you'll have anything
  of your choice.'

The boy looked at the princess and with a smile so
    grand:
'If I succeed at your request I'll have your
    daughter's hand.'

The Emperor was pleased; for him a small price to
    pay.
He told the guards to release the boy and sent him
    on his way.
'I have an empire and a palace, but still it's not
    enough.
I must have more riches and lots of shiny stuff.'

The boy set off that day across the desert sand,
Walked many miles to a strange enchanted land.
As he stopped to rest a magic river did appear,
The boy could not believe his eyes and he was filled
    with fear.

On the far side of the bank, a small creature he
    could see,
The creature looked straight back at him, 'What do
    you want from me?'
'I expected perhaps a genie or even a witch or two,
I'm not even sure what I'm looking at, what on
    earth are you?'

The creature sprouted wings and flew with a gentle
    buzzing.
'I'm a nymph of the magic river, I am a genie's
    cousin.'

'I must take you to the Emperor as he did spare my life,
Then when I get back to him, I'll take his daughter for my wife.'

'I know the Emperor that you speak of, my cousin helped him out,
He says that he will keep his word, this I truly doubt.
When you return back to his kingdom, I'm sure he'll have you jailed
And your quest to find true love surely will have failed.'

The boy stood up and rubbed his head, 'I'll beat him at his own game,
I beg of you now, good nymph, can you tell me my name?'
'Indeed I can, Your Highness, you are the prince of a distant land,
I shall tell your name in full when you take your princess by the hand.'

They had to get back to the Emperor so the nymph called a giant eagle.
They climbed upon the eagle's back and took off flying regal.
Returning to the palace after nearly an hour's flight,
They landed in the courtyard ready for a fight.

The Emperor and his daughter were quick to come and see

The orphan boy and magic nymph arrive like fantasy.
The Emperor called out, 'Now I'll have his power,
Hand over the river nymph and I'll throw you in the tower.'

The boy strode forward, raised his hand, 'Just wait Your Majesty,
The nymph has something for you, just you wait and see!'
The river nymph threw magic at the Emperor and his daughter,
The princess remained beautiful but the Emperor was now a pauper.

'Things are back to normal, the way that things should be,
Now it's time to take your bride with a little help from me.'
The couple married quickly, the river nymph then said
'Your name in full as promised, you are now Prince Ted.'

Pixie Battle

Elves and gnomes together, not at all at ease,
Then you throw in pixies and the trouble comes in
  threes.
Dwarves join in the melee and giants make it hairy,
Then the numbers double when you count up all
  the fairies.

The battle was impressive, on a scale so grand,
Luckily it happened down in Fairy-tale Land.
The giants were the favourites, all strong as a horse,
But the fairies flew rings around them, throwing
  them off course.

The gnomes were well-honed soldiers, fighting as a
  troop
Ably assisted by a little elf help group.
The pixies were the odd ones out, battling on their
  own,
But they were doing really well, especially with the
  gnomes.

The giants were getting tired, although they're big
  and strong,
With fairies flying around them, they couldn't keep
  it up for long.

A pixie got isolated but did well by himself;
He was very proud, beating up an elf.

But the elf would be all right, ready for adventure,
Given a week to recuperate in a small elf centre.
No one won the battle, they all decided to go home;
Except for all the pixies, they chose to go gnome
    sweet gnome.

Billy Bob and Betty Sue

There was a naughty brother and sister,
Billy Bob and Betty Sue.
Whatever naughty Billy did,
Betty would do too.
But she would do it bigger,
And better than before;
That's the only way she was sure
She could even up the score.

Billy cut a tree down,
Betty knocked down a wall.
Billy put his skates on the stairs,
Betty made dad fall.
Billy pulled the tree-house down,
Betty set the thing on fire.
Billy tried to put the fire out,
Betty made the flames go higher.

They never paid attention
And they broke all of the rules.
They were always in detention
For being naughty when at school.
Billy turned all the taps on,
He thought that it was good.
Betty went a step too far
And made the classroom flood.

They let the air out of the tyres
Of all the teachers' cars.
Then they went to a sweet shop
And opened all the jars.
Billy went into the garden
And pulled up all the roses.
Betty went to nursery
And pinched their little noses.

Billy was a bully
To all the little boys.
Betty made it even worse
By breaking all their toys.
Betty would knock on doors,
Then they both would run.
They'd giggle round the corner,
Having loads of fun.

He threw stones at windows,
But she would make them smash.
He liked to go pushing trolleys
And she would make them crash.
He would go to the cinema
And talk through all the features,
While she would throw water bombs
At all their friends and teachers.

Billy liked to roll in mud
While he wore his Sunday best.
Betty liked her best clothes
To have more holes than all the rest.
Billy liked to make prank calls

Up and down the land.
Betty did it further
When she phoned the Netherlands.

Billy liked to wear his shoes
On opposing feet.
Betty wore her daddy's shoes,
Didn't she look sweet.
Billy would do the crossword
Before anyone had read the paper,
But Betty cut the pictures out,
What a cheeky caper.

Billy would stay awake at night
Until his eyes were red.
Betty wouldn't get up next day,
She wouldn't leave her bed.
Billy liked to kick his ball
Into other peoples' homes.
Betty liked to go in too
And break their little gnomes.

While she was in the garden,
She'd pull up all the flowers
While Billy played his music loud
Into the early hours.
Billy Bob and Betty Sue,
You'll often hear it said:
The only time that they are good
Is when they're asleep in bed!

The Queen and the Stable Boy

In days of old when men were bold
And knights wore shining armour,
The stable boy had seen the Queen
And thought he'd try to charm her.
But who was he? It was plain to see
There could be no romance.
She was the Queen and although he was keen
It really gave them no chance.
He was a bit shy but he'd caught her eye
So he thought it good to give it a try.

He threw in his name and entered the games
And climbed on his mighty steed.
He sat on his horse, set it on course
And set off at a high rate of speed.
Charging at each other, two mighty noble knights,
The jousting competition, only one could win the fight.
After the hit, the farm boy took it, happy he was standing.
The knight was down upon the ground, he'd had a heavy landing.
Watched by the hordes, next came the swords,
The stable boy determined to win.

He gave it his best and struck at the chest
Then raised his arms with a grin.

It remained to be seen if he'd meet the Queen,
There was only one more fight.
Archery it was, he liked it because the Queen
   was in his sight.
He fired his arrow, smooth and narrow,
It soared straight and true.
With a thud that was dull it was into the bull,
Nothing more he could do.
The knight took his shot, gave it all that he'd
   got
But he totally missed.
The knight had come second,
The stable boy beckoned.
The Queen and the stable boy kissed.

Joey and the Monsters

Joey wasn't happy, it was nearly time for bed,
He was sulking in the bath with bubbles round his
head.
It was very nearly time when his mum turns out the
light,
That's when the monsters come and give him such
a fright.
He got into his jammies and then he kissed his
mum.
'Please don't turn the lights off, that's when the
monsters come.'
His mum looked at him and smiled, 'There's no
need to fear.'
She had a quick look around. 'See, no monsters
here.'

She kissed him on the forehead and tucked him in
so tight,
But Joey was afraid as she turned out the light.
He pulled his covers close and then sat up in bed
Waiting for the monsters and hoping they'd been
fed.
Then his wardrobe creaked and his curtains began
to blow.
Joey looked around him, where did his mummy go?

Then he started shaking at the noise his wardrobe
   made.
His drawers started to open and he was so afraid.
The monsters started coming, really scary guys,
Joey was so afraid he couldn't close his eyes.
With monsters coming closer, Joey thought it was a
   dream,
But then he knew it wasn't and so started to scream.

His mum came in the room and she turned on the
   light.
Joey looked around, not a thing in sight.
His mother left the room and turned the light off
   once again.
The monsters started stirring, Joey closed his eyes
   and then,
'Hello, my name is Marvin. These are all my
   friends.
I'm sorry that we scared you. We do that now and
   then.'

Joey rubbed his eyes, there at the foot of his bed,
A scaly, slimy monster with a giant, hairy head.
All around his room there were lots of things about,
Some were big, some were small and more kept
   coming out.
'We don't like it here, all locked up inside,
Climb onto my back and we'll take you for a ride.'
Joey climbed aboard, his windows opened to the
   night,
One by one the monsters flew and Marvin then
   took flight.

Up and down among the clouds, soaring high and
low,
The monsters flew on happily, nowhere they
couldn't go.
Joey wasn't scared, he was having so much fun,
Then the trip was over, the pleasure ride was done.
They took Joey back home and tucked him into
bed,
Marvin turned the light off, 'Good night,' the
monster said.
Then the monsters disappeared as the sun began to
rise;
Joey snuggled up in bed and closed his weary eyes.

He'd not been asleep for long, his mum came after a
while,
She gently started waking him and looked down
with a smile.
'Were there any monsters?' his mummy asked and
grinned.
'Don't be silly Mummy, there isn't such a thing.'

Vax

I'll tell you about a person,
You'll really get to hate her;
Smelly little tramps were the only ones to date her.
Her name, you'll think I'm joking, was Victoria
Applejax.
Her friends, only a few that there were, preferred to
call her Vax.
Now Vax she was a cheat, and whenever playing
poker,
She'd give up being with the King and run off with
the joker.
She turned her back on everyone that tried to make
life good,
She walked all over family and was as rotten as she
could.
She had no time for children and enjoyed setting
cars on fire,
Another thing she liked to do: she was a rotten little
liar.
She only was a short girl, some would say a gnome;
Everybody hated her, that's why she lived alone.

The Comic Book Kid

Pete loved reading comics, it's how he spent his days,
When he went to bed at night he'd let imagination
run away.
He'd cuddle up under his covers and close his tired
eyes,
Then wear a coloured costume and soar among the
skies.
A hero to the world, famed for doing good,
He'd fly around the world doing everything he could.

One night as he was dreaming, an evil came to play,
It was up to Super Pete to come and save the day.
But this time it was different, the Dream Demon
was real,
If Pete got hurt while dreaming, in real life he
wouldn't heal.
But Pete was unaware, arriving as a hero would,
He presumed he was immune as he tried to do
some good.

He soared down from the heavens, flying without a
sound,
The Dream Demon lashed out at him and struck
him to the ground.

Pete stood straight back up, he'd never been hit so
  hard,
His sleeping body back in bed, his shoulder was
  now scarred.
Super Pete kept flying and attacked him round the
  head;
He was struck down once again, his body bruised in
  bed.

Pete looked at the demon, his eyes burning it with
  flame,
The demon stood and took it, that's when the big
  shock came.
Super Pete had gone, but Pete was now awake.
His mum had heard him dreaming and thought it
  best to give a shake.
Although he was really tired, Pete didn't want to
  sleep.
His body ached all over and he was in trouble
  deep.

But there was nothing for it, he had to settle down,
Then Super Pete was back, flying over town.
The demon was on a rampage, he could hear
  civilians scream.
Then Pete had an idea, after all it was his dream.
Without warning, another demon he had made.
The Dream Demon looked at it and then it was
  afraid.

It screamed out really loud and in a cloud of smoke
It simply disappeared, and that's when Pete awoke.

He was wide awake, it was the middle of the night,
He couldn't wait to get back to sleep and have
  another fight.

Father and Son

A dark stormy night at the castle in the fens,
Creatures came out of the swamp, the king had no defence.
Merging with the rain, they approached the castle wall.
A few brave soldiers gave a fight but soon they all would fall.
The king was taken captive but his son made it away,
He would raise an army and return again one day.

The prince's name was Michael, a brave man he was at heart,
But it made him cry inside with the king and he apart.
On that day he made a vow: an army he would bring;
He would beat the creatures to the ground and release his beloved king.
So he then set off, Prince Michael of the Fens,
To search across the land to find some worthy men.

For two long years he searched, looking up and down,
Finding archers, fighters and swordsmen in every village and town.

The king was in the dungeon, one night he had a
    vision:
He'd seen a missing loved one release him from his
    prison.
It gave him hope, it made him strong,
He knew his son would not be long.

In all the time they held him, the creatures never said
    a thing,
They seemed not to know of his son or the army he
    would bring.
Their leader was called Ingar, an immortal it was
    told.
He'd been born before the Earth but no one knew
    how old.
No one knew how to kill him, if any way at all,
But Michael would have to find a way to make the
    creature fall.

An army on the move, Michael and his men,
Marching with a mission to the castle in the fens.
Just like two years ago, another rainy night,
The army came in under darkness ready for a fight.
The creatures on the lookout didn't hear a thing,
Arrows easily found their mark; the creatures felt
    their sting.

The drawbridge got pulled down and the army
    marched on through;
The creatures were surprised, they didn't have a
    clue.

Then the onslaught started and the creatures came
  in hordes,
The night illuminated by the sparks from clashing
  swords.
Fights were happening everywhere as arrows filled
  the sky,
Michael leading from the front with his royal battle
  cry.

Ingar heard the noise and came out with his axe.
Soldiers tried to get to him but fell as they attacked.
Ingar joined the battle with his axe above his head,
Michael saw him coming, he wouldn't rest till he
  was dead.
Michael battled through and archers cleared his
  path.
Axe versus sword, it was time to feel his wrath!

The axe came crashing down, Michael dodging it
  with ease,
Striking with his sword, bringing Ingar to his knees.
He stabbed him in the chest but Ingar rose back to
  his feet.
The power of immortals, how can he be beat?
Michael took a step back, unsure what could be
  done,
So he turned around and Ingar watched him run.

The battle kept on raging, Michael so far had failed.
He ran down to the dungeon where he found his
  father jailed.
He had a look around and found the prison key,

Undid his father's bonds and quickly set him free.
Father and son together they ran back to the fight,
Battling through the hordes till they had Ingar in
sight.

Ingar saw them coming and prepared to take a
stand.
Michael raised his sword and took his father's hand.
Ingar's axe came crashing down, slicing through the
men,
But they both stood up unscathed, Ingar watched
and then
Michael and the king raised their arms much higher
And from their raised hands came a magic fire.

Ingar went up in flames, his immortal power done.
There's no greater power than love of father for his
son.

Then and To Come

They said that he was crazy,
They told him he was a fool,
His ideas they said were stupid,
They laughed him out of school.
But look who's laughing now –
That's Professor Lionel Grace.
I've been the one to help him,
To help him save his face
We worked well together
Between us we got work done.
But now the time was here
To do a trial run.

The Professor worked the computer
While I checked the invention,
The Chronomap Transporter!
It was a name he'd forgot to mention.
I strapped myself in tight,
Pulled the canopy overhead.
Professor Grace gave me a thumbs up,
'*1914!*' I think he said.

I'm not quite sure what happened
But something sure went wrong.
When I was travelling back in time,
It went on for far too long.

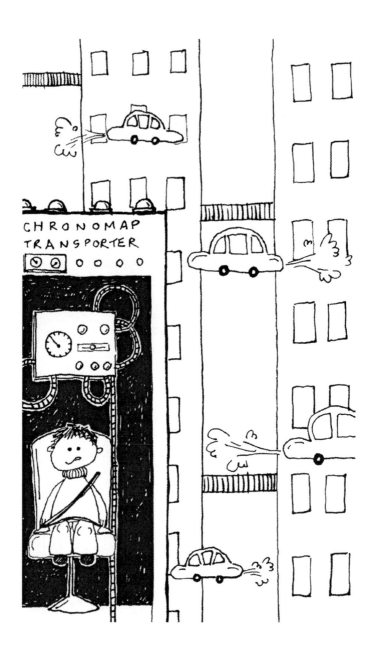

I should have just arrived
At the beginning of the war,
But as I looked around
I could not believe the things I saw.

Everywhere around me,
There were dinosaurs abound.
Some flying in the air
While volcanoes shook the ground.
Sixty-five million years,
That's how far I'd travelled to the past.
I had to find my way home
And I had to do it fast
Because I could see just ahead,
Coming through the trees,
A huge tyrannosaurus coming after me.

I had to leave the Transporter
And run to stay alive,
But the dinosaur kept coming,
How could I survive?
Suddenly out of nowhere,
A triceratops joined the fray,
It charged at the tyrannosaurus
And let me get away.
Then as I kept running,
Something caught my eye,
A soaring pterodactyl
Coming at me from the sky.

I hid behind a rock,
The ptera passed on by,

Lucky it hadn't seen me
So I stood and watched it fly.
Then I took a moment
Just to take a look around,
To see all the wondrous creatures
That the time machine had found.

I saw brontos in the water
And stegos eating leaves.
In the air high above me,
Pterodactyls on the breeze.
It was at this point I realized,
I was in a place I'd never seen.
Before I wandered off too far,
I must find the time machine.

So I turned around
And tried to retrace my steps,
Hoping the triceratops
Had seen off the tyrannosaurus rex.
But pretty soon I'd found it
And it all seemed to be together;
Now it was time to go home
Or be lost in time forever.
I climbed into the cockpit
And set the dials for two thousand seven,
But it sent me to the future
To the year three thousand seven.

The whole place was illuminated
By an artificial light.
There was no way of telling

If it was day or it was night.
It was as though the world was crazy,
I would have to leave here soon.
Looking to the sky,
There was neither sun nor moon.
Everyone was walking round
With a mask upon their face,
They looked me up and down,
I must have seemed so out of place.
Cars hovered overhead
And buildings floated on air,
Dogs took themselves for walks
And all the walls were bare.
The whole area seemed so sterile,
Without a human touch;
I had a longing to go home,
I missed the place so much.

Resetting all the dials,
I kept my fingers crossed,
I had to make it home this time
Or be forever lost.
The machine began to buzz,
Lights began to flash.
I felt solid ground underneath
As I landed with a crash.
I opened up the canopy,
Glad to see a familiar face,
Because there smiling back at me
Was Professor Lionel Grace.

I told him of the dinosaurs
And my adventures in the past.
Then I told him of the future
And how it would never last.

Illegally Human

It hadn't been a good one,
It had been a dismal day.
He'd been fired from his job
And his girlfriend walked away.

Walking down the street,
Feeling all the pain.
Nothing else could go wrong,
Then he felt the rain.

He pulled his collar up
And tucked his hands in tight;
Trying to claim some warmth
From the coldness of the night.

He was deeply lost in thought
And the rain kept falling down.
This was when he realized
He was in the darker side of town.

Derelict old buildings
With windows cracked and smashed.
Here he took his shelter
As thunder rolled and lightning flashed.

Looking up at darkened skies,
There was another lightning flash.
Then somewhere behind him,
He heard an echoed smash.

Turning with a shock,
He went to take a look.
Thunder rolling once again,
The entire building shook.

There amongst the darkness
Of an ever blacker night,
Creeping from a doorway,
He could just make out a light.

Moving through the shadows,
He wanted to know more.
He had to know what was going on
So he moved closer to the door.

He pushed the door wide open,
Almost blinded by the light.
There spread out in front of him,
An unexpected sight.

He almost fainted on a table,
It was the nearest thing to grab.
Everywhere around him
Was a scientific lab.

There were chemicals in jars
And computers round the walls.
A gigantic cryo-chamber
At the centre of it all.

He walked up to the chamber
And took a look within.
Then before he knew it,
Someone pushed him in.

The door easily opened,
He stepped out feeling strange.
He had a look around him,
Everything had changed.

Something must have happened,
Nothing here was right.
The lab was filthy dirty,
No longer sparkling white.

He took a step outside,
Gone were all the clouds.
It was now middle of the day,
Where were all the crowds?

The streets were all deserted,
Not a soul in sight.
How long had he been gone?
What happened to the night?

A paper blew close by him,
He grabbed it and read the year.
This surely could not have happened,
There's no way he could be here.

He stopped and read the headlines,
His mouth open wide in awe;
Aliens had taken over,
Being human now against the law.

One hundred years had gone,
A century he had lost.
He must now find survivors
No matter what the cost.

Before he could react
Aliens surrounded him so fast.
The ground shook him off his feet
With a well-placed laser blast.

'You are recognised as **Human**,
Therefore under arrest.'
He struggled to his feet
With a laser at his chest.

He held out his hands,
Waiting to be bound.
Suddenly an explosion!
It knocked them to the ground.

He quickly set off running,
Ready for the chase.
Ducking round the corner,
He saw a friendly face.

Eight faces in total
And he was happy to be found.
A misfit group of renegades,
They called themselves **The Underground**.

They took him into hiding,
Way down in the sewers.
They told him of their plans
To defeat the alien evildoers.

There was a manufacturing plant
On the northern side of town.
They were planning on breaking in
To burn the factory down.

Later that same evening,
Under cover of the night,
Hiding in the shadows,
Ready for a fight.

The factory made masks
For aliens everywhere.
If they didn't wear them,
They couldn't breathe Earth's air.

The aliens were unprepared,
Not ready for an attack.
The **Underground** ran riot
As they took their planet back.

The factory went up,
With flames up to the sky,
And all around the world
The aliens began to die.

He too was now a renegade,
Part of **The Underground**,
Happy to start rebuilding
With these new friends he'd found.

Joey and the Snowman

The middle of a cold, dark winter,
It had been a frosty night.
Joey opened up his curtains,
All the ground was white.
Jack Frost had covered his window,
Why, he didn't know.
He just wanted to get outside
And play in all the snow.

He quickly dashed downstairs
With a smile upon his face,
Put on his wellies, gloves and hat
And out the door he raced.
Falling to the floor,
A snow angel he made.
Rolling in the snow,
Happily he played.

Joey rolled up a big ball,
Then another one slightly smaller,
Placed it on top of the other
To make his snowman taller.
He gave it black coal eyes
And a carrot nose upon its face;
A little pebble smile
He then gently placed.

He gave the snowman a hug
And told him he was loved,
Then he dashed inside
To remove his coat and gloves.
Little did he know
That the love he had to give
Had brought the snowman real life
And he began to live.

A couple of hours later,
Joey came back out to play.
There was no sign of his snowman,
It had simply gone away.
He looked around his house
And checked inside his shed,
There he found his snowman,
He looked at it and said,
'How did you get here?
What are you doing inside?'
Imagine his surprise
When the snowman then replied,
'Hello Joey,' it said,
'I hope to be your friend,
But we don't have long together,
Just till the winter's end.'

Joey almost collapsed,
He couldn't believe what he'd just heard.
A snowman said hello to him,
This truly was absurd.
'How can this be happening?
It really can't be true.'

The snowman simply smiled at him,
'It's because you said "I love you".'

Joey started laughing,
He had a new best friend,
They could do so many things together,
But so little time to spend.
'Tell me, Mr Snowman,
Do you have a name?'
'Well, you are called Joey,
I think I'll be the same.'

Joey thought a moment,
'I think I'll call you Joe,
You can't be the same as me
Because you are made of snow.'
Joey said to his snowman,
'What happens next then, Joe?'
'I'm made purely out of water,
There's nowhere I cannot go.'

They took each other's hand
And disappeared down the drain.
A magic ride through pipes
And reappeared just like rain.
They were at the local park
Where they played on swings and slides.
Then it was the time
For another magic ride.

All through the winter
They went to so many different places,

Saw so many things
And shocked so many faces.
But the snowman started shrinking,
Getting smaller day by day.
Then it finally happened,
He just melted away.

Joey missed his friend
And couldn't help but shed a tear,
But he remembered what the snowman said:
'I'll be back again next year!'

Donny Dunn

The roughest, toughest cop in town,
Donny Dunn they called him.
He thought he did his job quite well
But his captain soon would have him hauled in.
'But it only took one shot,' he really did protest,
'I couldn't miss from that close range,
I did it for the best.'
The captain took a big, deep breath,
'Dunn, you'll be the death of me.
You shouldn't have had to draw your gun
To get that cat out of the tree!'

Later that afternoon,
There was a hold-up at a shop.
Shots were fired in the air
And the call went out for cops.
Arriving with a screech of brakes,
Having already drawn his gun,
The robbers knew they would be caught
Because here comes Donny Dunn!
He opened up his boot,
Took out a hand grenade.
He blew the entire shop up
Then admired the mess he'd made.

His reputation grew,
The baddest cop in all the land.
Whenever there was danger,
He'd be there with gun in hand.
And after he'd stopped the crisis
With his ever faithful gun,
They'd look at all the chaos
And say 'That's what Donny done!'

Dontgothere

You all remember Eve
And how she liked to walk around.
Now she'd heard of somewhere new,
It had only just been found.
Word had come from far and wide
To tell her how and where.
The name itself was a warning though,
It was simply called 'Dontgothere'.

But Eve was really interested
And she simply had to go.
What troubles lay in wait for her?
Eve didn't really know.
She packed her bags up once again
And set off without a care,
But the path was filled with danger
On the way to Dontgothere.

She came across a signpost,
Which way should she face?
One sign pointed to Dontgothere,
The other to Wasaplace.
She walked on down the path,
The sky started turning black
But she'd have to keep on going,
There was no turning back.

Then the heavy rain came
And Eve got soaked through to the bone.
'Come this way to dry off, my dear,'
Said a hairy little gnome.
Eve was shocked to see him
But he seemed to be a friend.
So she followed him down the path
And around a little bend.

As they came around the corner,
She could see a little home,
'This is where I live, my dear,'
Said the hairy little gnome.
'Thank you for your help, good sir,'
Eve introduced herself.
'You are welcome,' said the gnome
And took a jar down off the shelf.

Eve sat by the fire
Trying to get dry.
The gnome opened up the jar,
Out buzzed a dragonfly.
'How beautiful,' said Eve,
She complimented its colour.
'It used to be,' said the gnome,
'But now it's getting duller.
I found him when he was lost,
Now I think he's ill.
We've got to get him home,
Back to Dragonfly Hill.'

Eve happily agreed
And set off with the gnome.

She was always happy
When she had somewhere to roam.
Now, where was it she was going?
Dragonfly Hill? Not one she'd known.
'It's on the far side of Dontgothere,'
Explained the friendly little gnome.

The rain had long since stopped,
Eve felt warm and dry.
She saw as she looked around,
Flying unicorns in the sky.
A griffin crossed their path,
The gnome said it was lucky.
Eve was not so sure,
She wasn't feeling plucky.

They were getting near the outskirts
Of the town of Dontgothere.
The gnome saw that Eve was getting anxious,
He told her there's no reason to be scared.
The natives came out to see them,
Some had giant heads;
Some had spots and stripes,
Others were blue and red.

The gnome moved to the middle,
The entire town stood still.
They all listened to the gnome
As he asked for Dragonfly Hill.
The mayor of the town stepped forward,
Half dinosaur and half horse,
'Your dragonfly is ill,
We will help you, of course.'

They got a team together
Of the village's strongest men.
They headed off down the path
And through a flowery glen.
They arrived at Dragonfly Hill
After hours of walking around.
Dragonflies were everywhere,
In the air and on the ground.

The villagers spread out
They had changed their attitude,
'Eve, will you please forgive us
But we love dragonflies as food.'
They started catching them in nets,
Eve said they'd gone too far.
She dashed out to the middle
And took the lid off the glass jar.

The dragonfly flew loose
And started getting large.
He turned into a dragon,
Now he was the one in charge.
The villagers ran and fell
As all the dragons turned.
Only Eve and the gnome left standing,
Nearly everyone else got burned.

The others ran away
And some dragons gave them chase.
Eve turned towards the dragon King,
It was the one from Wasaplace.
But that dragon was a man,

The spell was broken, Eve had seen.
Yet they were both here
As the dragon king and queen.

The king moved closer to her
'Eve, our thanks again.
Another spell is broken
Placed on us by those men.
We like it here as dragons,
It's a really peaceful life.
I enjoy it as a ruler
Sitting here with my wife.'

They told them of a new path home,
One that went around Dontgothere.
The gnome and Eve said together,
'Don't worry, we won't go there!'
Eve and the gnome walked off,
Relieved the day was through.
The dragons were living happily,
There was nothing more to do.

Eve then looked down
At the friendly little gnome,
'I hope you don't think me forward,
But may I walk you home?'
The gnome looked back up at her,
'I think best not my dear,
Because I live in a little town,
It's called **Youdbetternotbehere**!'

Joey and the Haunted House

Joey was having regrets
Because Joey was getting scared.
He wished that he'd said no
On the day that he'd been dared.

Spend the night in a haunted house
Was all he had to do.
Now things were moving around him,
Things that may go '*BOO!*'

When he'd first arrived
He said he wasn't afraid,
But that was well before
Noises were being made.

He was lying there in bed,
Suffering from fright;
Waiting for things to come,
Things that go bump in the night.

Then he heard another noise,
He heard the staircase creak.
Dare he go and look,
Is it worth a peak?

He edged closer to his door
And opened it just a bit
He was embarrassed to admit it
But he was scared out of his wits.

Through the murky darkness,
Within the growing gloom,
Joey saw something coming.
He ran back inside his room.

He fell across the floor
And rolled under his bed.
Ghostly, ghastly visions
Floating in his head.

He saw the door pushed open
And something came inside.
Joey's teeth were chattering
As he did his best to hide.

But he had to take a look,
What had he to lose?
Hold on there one minute!
Since when did ghosts wear shoes?

Joey, now feeling brave,
Got up to his feet.
He walked towards the ghost
And took off a white sheet.

There standing before him
Was one of his friends from school.
He'd been trying to scare him,
Joey felt such a fool.

The two fell to the floor
Amidst the sound of laughter.
They didn't see the ghost
That was quickly reaching after.

Joey turned around
And saw a glowing face.
He and his friend then ran
Away quickly from that place.

Running down the stairs,
The door they tried to find,
Going quickly as they could,
The ghost not far behind.

They ran down a corridor
And down some darkened halls;
With a ghost hot on their trail,
It seemed to pass through walls.

They ran into the lounge
With no place left to go,
And all around the doorway
There came an eerie glow.

There was nowhere they could run.
What more could they do?
The ghosts came in the room.
There wasn't one but two!

Then the ghosts removed their sheets,
The boys were now very glad
Because underneath the glowing sheets
Was Joey's mum and dad!